CW00525378

The Ultimate Air Fryer Cookbook:

2000 Days of Effortless, Budget-Friendly, and Flavorful
Culinary Creations | Beginner-Friendly Instructions for
Delightful Meals

By:
Myron Wind

© Copyright 2023 - All rights reserved.

The author or publisher must give written permission to reproduce, duplicate, or transmit this book.

The publisher and author are not liable for any damages, recovery, or financial loss resulting from this book's information. Neither directly nor indirectly.

Legal Notice:

This book is copyrighted. This book is personal only. This book cannot be modified, distributed, sold, used, quoted, or paraphrased without the author's or publisher's permission.

Disclaimer Notice:

The information in this document is for educational and entertainment purposes only. All efforts were made to present accurate, current, reliable, and complete information. No guarantees are made. Readers agree that the author does not provide legal, financial, medical, or professional advice. Text in this book comes from various sources. Before using any of this book's techniques, consult a licensed professional.

The reader agrees that the author is not liable for any direct or indirect loss resulting from the use of this document's information, including errors, omissions, or inaccuracies.

Table of Contents

Chapter 6: Lunch Recipes 49

Chapter 7: Dinner Recipes 71

Introduction

Anyone can use the revolutionary Air Fryer, a kitchen appliance, to prepare delicious, healthy foods with just one click and little to no oil. It can be used as an oven and a fryer.

Due to their low calorie and fat content, air-fried foods are thought to be a better option than deep-fried ones. To achieve a flavor and texture like deep-fried foods, air-frying uses only a tablespoon of oil rather than fully submerging the food.

Food is fried using air fryers, which circulate hot air around the food as it is cooked. Because air-fried foods only require a small amount of oil to produce a similar texture and flavor to deep-fried foods, air-fried diets are thought to be healthier than deep-fried ones.

While air-fried foods can be less dangerous than deep-fried foods, it is important to remember that they are still foods that have been fried in oil.

Consuming fried foods may have a number of harmful health effects, according to numerous studies.

For instance, a study that involved 15,362 participants came to the conclusion that eating fried foods increases the risk of developing heart failure.

Recent research has discovered that regularly consuming deep-fried foods may increase your risk of developing certain cancers, such as breast, lung, and oral cancer.

Fried food consumption is frequently associated with diseases like type 2 diabetes and high blood pressure. Although air-fried foods have not been studied for their effects, using fried food to promote better health is advised.

Alternatively, to improve the flavor of fried food and prevent negative health effects, use safer cooking methods like roasting, baking, steaming, or sautéing. Air freezing may be healthier than deep frying, but frying has a number of negative health effects, including the development of heart disease, high blood pressure, diabetes, and other types of cancer.

Using an air fryer will reduce the amount of fat, calories, and potentially harmful compounds in your diet when compared to deep-fried foods. However, when cooked in oil and consumed frequently, air-fried foods are comparable to traditional fried foods and may be linked to harmful health conditions.

Reduce your intake of fried foods if you want to increase your safety, even though air fryers can be a safer alternative to deep fryers.

Features of An Air Fryer

Have you ever seen or used a convection oven that fits on a countertop? However, an air fryer has a much more powerful convection system that forces hot air through the food at a much faster rate. Other than that, its operation is very similar to that of a standard deep fryer. Because of the way that it was designed, the food can be placed in a sealed chamber directly underneath the fan and close to the heating element that is located on the top. The following is a list of the primary components that can be found in every air fryer; these components work together to make air frying possible.

Air Fryer and the heating system:

An air fryer is essentially a cylindrical container that is sealed on all sides and has a heating element located at the very top. It also has a cooking chamber located at the very bottom. Because of the powerful convection created by the fan that is fixed underneath the heating element of the fryer, the heat is released from the top of the food and then circulates in the cooking chamber. This is in contrast to the majority of other cooking appliances. Your food is fried as a result of the heating element and the fan working together. In addition to this heating element, the machine has a thermostat that is connected to it. This thermostat is responsible for regulating the temperature that is present within the cooking chamber whenever heat is produced. The internal temperature is kept stable by the heating element, which operates in cycles.

Air Fryer Basket and the Fryer Drawer:

The Air Fryer's cooking chamber is nothing more than an empty area that houses a drawer that can be removed from the device. Using this drawer, one can easily add food to the air fryer while also maintaining control over it. This drawer has a handle on the outside, and a pull-out button on top of the handle that you need to press and pull in order to open it. If you don't do either of those things, the drawer stays locked and fixed in the air fryer. Instead of placing the food directly in the drawer, an air fryer basket is put in the drawer first, and then the food is placed in the basket. Because the base of the basket is porous, the hot air is able to move through the food in the basket with relative ease. The basket can be removed and cleaned in its own separate compartment. This basket can also be used for and stored a variety of other cooking utensils and accessories, including the following:

- Baking pan
- Casserole dish
- Ramekins
- Air fryer rack

Control Panel and Control dials:

There is a control panel that is present on the front top portion of an Air fryer. This control panel is usually designed to allow better control over time and temperature settings of the machine. There are two control dials present on the panel:

The temperature dial:

The temperature dial can be used to increase or decrease the temperature values on the control panel display. You can select any value from 175 F to 400 F.

The timer dial:

The dial on the timer can be turned to extend or shorten the amount of time that the food is allowed to cook for. On most air fryers, you'll find a timer dial with a fixed setting of sixty minutes.

Then there is a control panel display that indicates the various cooking processes that are taking place. It has a variety of lights, each of which corresponds to a different function. For example, there are typically the following:

The machine is producing usable output, as denoted by the presence of the red light.

When the function of heating or cooking is complete, the indicator light will turn blue.

Note that these are features that can be found in virtually all of the different models of air fryers. There are a number of additional side or optional features that are available in various new models of air fryers. These features are not discussed here because they are not relevant to the topic at hand.

What Kind Of Meals Can You Prepare?

People who were interested in eating healthier meals could benefit from oil-free, crispy food that could be prepared in an air fryer. On the other hand, as the use of air fryers became more widespread, new and improved applications for these devices emerged. As of right now, the menu features a wide variety of items that you are able to prepare using your air fryer, some of which are as follows:

All Crispy Snacks: Rolls, fries, fat bombs, crisps, etc.

Meals for breakfast include things like frittata, bread, omelets, bacon, and sausages.

Seafood and Fish: Crunchy coated cod, salmon, shrimp, and other seafood options.

Steaks, chops, drumettes, chicken wings, and other cuts of poultry and meat such as these.

Side Dishes and Main Dishes Comprised of Vegetables Crispy broccoli, Brussels sprouts, and cauliflower florets, potato cups, and a zucchini boat, etc.

Desserts and Fruits including things like muffins, soufflé, fried fruits, cookies, biscuits, and other similar items.

Air May be Safer Than Fryer

For traditional frying, food is submerged in hot oil and allowed to remain in the oil until it reaches the desired level of doneness, browning, and crispiness. In this method, you have to go the extra mile to remove all of the excess oil, and even then, there will always be some oil remaining in the food after it has been fried. Because of this, food that is cooked through regular frying typically has a higher content of fat, which is not always healthy, particularly for individuals who are suffering from high cholesterol or cardiac problems. In addition to that, dealing with oil frying can be a challenge. The use of hot oil presents a number of risks, and it also contaminates the surrounding area.

On the other hand, when you air fry, you don't need to worry about using any oil as a cooking medium. Instead of completely dipping or soaking the food in the oil, it is instead kept in a sealed chamber where hot air is passed under pressure. This causes the food to be cooked. The high temperature and high pressure of the air combine to produce a cumulative effect that fries the food from the outside, leaving it crispy and crunchy, whereas the overall temperature within the vessel cooks the food from the inside. Food can be prepared using the Air Fryer with a significantly reduced amount of oil or fat. Because all of the cooking takes place within the closed container, air frying is also good for the environment because it eliminates the need for grease in the surrounding area.

Foods that are fried in the oven tend to be more consistent than foods that are fried in oil due to a variety of factors.

These are lower in sugar and calorie content, as well as in certain compounds that may be unhealthy that are found in traditional fried foods. Switching to an air fryer could be a good option for you if you are having trouble losing weight or if you are increasing the amount of fat you consume without changing your diet or cutting back on fried foods.

Keep in mind, however, that just because it could be a healthier choice than deep-frying does not mean that it is a perfect alternative in terms of your overall wellbeing just because it is a healthier choice than deep-frying. Products that are air-fried are preferable because, in comparison to deep-fried food, they contain significantly less acrylamide, sugar, and calories. However, there are frequently fried foods available.

Chapter 1:
Benefits Of Air-Frying

Prepare to put what you are going to learn about fried foods to the test. Air fryers will fry your favorite foods to a fluffy, golden-brown perfection using very little to no gasoline at all (yes, this includes French fries and potato chips). Not only can you make traditional fried snacks like potato chips and French fries, but it's also great for fruits, proteins like chicken wings and drumettes, and appetizers like coquettes and feta triangles. This is because you can fry them in oil at a high temperature. Additionally, desserts such as brownies and blonds come out exquisitely cooked when prepared in an air fryer.

To put it another way, an air fryer is very similar to a convection oven, but it cooks food in a different manner by subjecting it to extremely high temperatures. Dry air, on the other hand, circulates around the food, causing it to be cooked more effectively while maintaining its crispiness without the need for any additional fat.

The air fryer is unequivocally an exceptional piece of cooking equipment. It makes it possible to prepare delicious food without having to use a lot of oil or fat. We experimented with a variety of techniques and recipes in an effort to improve the nutritional value of our go-to meals without sacrificing the dishes' signature crunch or flavor. This was important to us both financially and environmentally. Consumers are drawn to the instant air fryer because it has a number of features that make it convenient and appealing to use. The following is a sample of what we talked about earlier.

Portable: This cooking utensil can be taken with you. The air fryer is designed to be moved quickly and easily from the storage cabinet in your kitchen to the countertop or to another location.

The air fryer's automatic temperature control ensures that the food comes out of the appliance perfectly cooked every time.

With the air fryer's digital touch screen, you won't need to spend time mastering complicated cooking techniques because the appliance was designed with ease of use in mind. Cooking a wide variety of dishes is as simple as making a few taps on the screen of the touch panel. Thanks to the timer and buzzer, you won't have to worry about overcooking your food. Both the timer and the buzzer will alert you when the food is ready to be served.

Advice on Making the Most of Your Air Fryer

Your cravings can be satiated with foods that are crispier if you use an air fryer. To help you get the most out of your air fryer, here are some wonderful tips that you can use!

Move it around!

Be sure to open the fryer and shake the contents of the basket occasionally while they are "frying" in order to ensure even cooking. Compression may occur in foods of a smaller size, such as chips and French fries. Even if a recipe does not specifically instruct you to rotate, shake, or flip the food at regular intervals, you should still do so for the best possible results.

Do not make it too crowded.

Be sure to leave plenty of space around the food you are cooking to allow the hot air to effectively circulate around what you are doing. The results will be as crispy as you've been wishing for if you do this! In addition to that, it is best to work in relatively small batches.

Spritz your food.

The majority of recipes will instruct you to do so, but in the event that they don't, it is a good idea to spray the food with a little bit of oil lightly so that it does not stick to the basket while it is cooking. I would recommend purchasing a kitchen spray bottle that is large enough to hold oil. It is much simpler to use a spray on foods rather than completely covering them in this greasy substance.

Keep yourself dry.

Before placing foods in the air fryer basket, you need to ensure that they are thoroughly patted dry. Spattering and excessive smoking are both avoided as a result of this measure. Therefore, allow foods that have been marinated to drain a little bit before adding them, and when you are finished cooking foods that are high in fat content, make sure to empty the fat from the bottom of the fryer.

Acquire expertise in the use of various cooking methods

The air fryer can be used for more than just frying! It works wonderfully for a variety of alternative cooking methods, including grilling, roasting, and even baking! For the salmon with the best flavor, I always use this kitchen appliance.

When preparing fatty foods, add water to the pot.

By placing some water in the drawer that is located underneath the basket, you will reduce the risk of smoke filling your kitchen as a result of the grease that is found in foods that are higher in fat content. Make sure to do this in particular with burgers, sausage, and bacon.

Toothpicks are used to keep food in place.

Your air fryer may occasionally pick up foods that are light and blow them around the fryer as they are being cooked. Toothpicks can be used to keep foods you cook together.

You can access it whenever you like.

When you cook with an air fryer, one of the best advantages is that you do not have to worry about how frequently you have to open it up to check whether or not the food is done.

If you are a nervous cook, this can help you relax so that you can produce delicious meals and snacks each and every time.

Before removing the food, remove the basket first.

If you try to invert the air fryer basket while it is still securely locked in the drawer, you will end up wasting all of the fat that has been rendered from the food.

After each use, clean the drawer thoroughly.

The drawer of the air fryer is very simple to clean and requires very little effort overall. If you do not wash it, however, you run the risk of contaminating the food you cook in the future as well as having a foul odor permeate your entire kitchen. To avoid this problem, you need only clean it after each use.

To ensure that the appliance is dry, use the air dryer.

When you have finished cleaning the basket and the drawer of the air fryer, you can replace them in the fryer and then turn on the appliance for two to three minutes. This is an excellent method for thoroughly drying it in preparation for the subsequent use!

Let's move on to the scrumptious dishes you'll be able to prepare with an air fryer now that you have a better understanding of how the appliance operates. Because the book contains so many different recipes, you can be sure that whatever you make will be something that you and all of your loved ones can appreciate for the rest of your lives.

Chapter 2:
Air Fryer Tips & Tricks

Preheat the air fryer before placing the food inside

Even if you're going to cook something in the oven, you still give it a few minutes to warm up. An air fryer uses the same procedure. In the heated environment, food will taste more delicious. Despite this, many people overlook this straightforward step. Therefore, keep in mind how crucial it is to pay attention to this advice.

Grease the air fryer basket with some oil to prevent it from sticking

Even though many air fryers have a nonstick layer, it is still important to grease the device in order to prevent any problems from occurring. The oils that have a high smoking point and are suitable for use in high temperatures are without a doubt the ideal choice for the basket of an air fryer (such as soybean or safflower oil).

Extra hint: I strongly advise you to steer clear of extra-virgin varieties that smoke between 3,500 and 4,100 degrees Fahrenheit. Despite this, you can still use light types that smoke at temperatures ranging from 3900 to 4700 degrees Fahrenheit.

Use oil sparingly to achieve the best crispy food level

It is a common misconception that making food crispier in the machine by first soaking it in a significant amount of oil before putting it in the machine. It is important for you to understand that the amount of oil used does not affect the crispiness of the food. In addition, dipping your food in an excessive amount of oil can make it soggy rather than crisp, depending on the food.

Add spices to the oil before spreading them over the food

There are a lot of people who are unaware of the fact that this machine has exceptionally powerful air circulation. Because of this, certain lightweight spices can easily be blown off. Follow the instructions in the heading and combine some spices with the oil if you want to avoid that happening. Spices and herbs will remain adhered to the food as long as the oil is present.

Avoid using nonstick aerosol spray to prevent damaging your air fryer

Many individuals are unaware that cooking sprays designed to prevent sticking may contain additives. These additives have the potential to cause damage to the layer of your machine that prevents sticking. Because of this, make sure you steer clear of them. You can, however, find an excellent replacement for what you're looking for. You can put your oil in a spray bottle that you purchase and then use.

Leave at least five inches of space around your air fryer

Many individuals are unaware that cooking sprays designed to prevent sticking may contain additives. These additives have the potential to cause damage to the layer of your machine that prevents sticking. Because of this, make sure you steer clear of them. You can, however, find an excellent replacement for what you're looking for. You can put your oil in a spray bottle that you purchase and then use.

Don't overcrowd your air fryer

If you put an excessive amount of food into the basket of your air fryer, you will create a significant amount of chaos. When there are too many items inside of the air fryer, it will not function correctly. There will be a disruption in the air circulation, and the food won't have the same delicious flavor. Cooking food in an air fryer requires working in small batches if you need to prepare a large quantity of food at once. By preparing the food in this manner, you can ensure that it will become crispy. Always keep this piece of advice in mind, but especially when you are preparing french fries.

Cook large items in a single layer without stacking

If you want to prepare something like a whole chicken, steak, fish fillets, burgers, or pork chops, you should place them in one layer instead of stacking. It is necessary to follow this advice because you will not get what you expect. The parts that are touching will be soggy and colorless. Don't rush. Cook them in batches.

Add some water to the air fryer when you cook fatty food to prevent potential smoking

Foods high in fat, such as bacon, burgers, meatballs, and other similar items, may cause your new machine to start smoking. The fat collects in the basket of the air fryer and causes it to heat up. In the event that this occurs to you, you will need to turn off the air fryer, empty out the accumulated fat, and begin the process of cooking from the very beginning again. You can, however, prevent this from happening by beginning the cooking process in the air fryer with some water.

Don't forget to shake the basket during cooking

You can guarantee that everything in the basket will be cooked uniformly if you shake the basket at least a couple of times while it is in the oven. It comes in especially handy when preparing less substantial meals. Everything will achieve a crispy texture this way, including bite-sized pieces of vegetables and fries. You don't need to overdo it; just a few shakes will accomplish what needs to be done.

Instead of using the microwave, preheat your food in the air fryer

In the event that you have any leftovers, you can put them in the air fryer to reheat them. You don't have to do that in the microwave if you don't want to. You can reheat anything in your new machine, whether it be pizza, some vegetables, or chicken. You can even do all of these things at the same time. I will give you the recommendation to set the temperature to 350 degrees Fahrenheit. Because of this, the temperature has been set lower than usual to avoid the risk of your food becoming overcooked. After waiting for approximately one minute, you will be able to enjoy your leftovers in the same crisp and hot manner as you did the day before.

Cook any frozen food in the air fryer

Any frozen food, such as chicken nuggets or cauliflower gnocchi, can be cooked in an air fryer if the user so chooses. Check out our "Air Fryer Cooking Chart" if you are unsure of the temperature or amount of time needed for the cooking process.

You can toast nuts in the air fryer

Because it has a hot circulation, the air fryer can assist you in the process of toasting nuts. The process of getting ready is not complicated in any way. You then toss them into the basket and wait for them to turn golden and begin making popping sounds, which is an indication that they are finished.

Use drippings that accumulate in the drawer

These drippings, such as bacon fat drops, can be utilized in the preparation of various sauces and gravies. The fat that has been collected in the basket is perfectly usable and can be seasoned with a variety of flavors. Next time, rather than throwing it away, I suggest you put the mixture in a jar and store it that way. When you have some free time, make some gravies, sauces, or other dishes as you see fit.

Use parchment paper or foil to make cleaning quicker and easier

By placing some aluminum foil or parchment paper inside the basket before adding the food, you can help yourself avoid having to clean the basket for no reason after cooking particularly messy foods. Even if you use it to prepare foods that are high in grease, your air fryer will not get dirty.

Clean the air fryer after every use

It should not be cleaned in the dishwasher. Before attempting to clean the air fryer, give it some time to cool down. After that, you will need to clean the machine from top to bottom, including the basket, the drawer, and the entire apparatus. If there is smoke coming from your air fryer, you should not feel alarmed. That merely indicates that there is an accumulation of oil within your machine, which needs to be cleaned up. The following text will provide you with a step-by-step guide that will show you how you should clean it and what you will need to complete the process.

Chapter 3:

How to Clean the Air Fryer

There are some rules you should follow if you want to maintain your air fryer properly:

- Things like metal utensils, steel wire brushes, or abrasive sponges can only cause damage. Don't use them for removing food leftovers from the basket of the air fryer.
- Avoid sinking the air fryer in the water to clean it. You can damage your machine because it is electric.

How to clean the air fryer after each use

After each use of an air fryer, the basket, the pan, and the tray need to be cleaned thoroughly. When it comes to cleaning, using soap and water that is warm is your best bet. You should quickly clean the interior by using a cloth that is damp and to which a small amount of soap has been added. After you have finished the cleaning process, make sure that each component of the air fryer is completely dried.

It is a good idea to check the heating coil for oil on a regular basis. In the event that you notice some accumulation there, you will need to wait until the device has completely cooled down before cleaning it.

How to deep clean the air fryer

For deep cleaning, you need to be more careful and follow instructions. Let's start with the list of things you will need:

- Damp microfiber cloth or a non-abrasive sponge
- Soft-bristle scrub brush
- Baking soda
- Dish soap
- Dry, clean cloth

Now, follow the below instructions:

1. Turn off your electric device and let it cool down for about a half an hour without the plug in. Never clean a fryer that uses warm air.
2. Take the pan and the basket out of the air fryer, and then wash both of them in hot water with some dish soap. If you find that these components have some grease on them, soak them in hot water for approximately ten minutes, and then scrub them with a sponge that is not abrasive.
3. Use the soft, nonabrasive sponge to scrub the inside of the container with dishwashing liquid. Use a fresh damp cloth to remove it completely.
4. Invert the machine so that it is standing on its back, and then use a sponge or a damp cloth to thoroughly clean each of the heating elements.

5. You can use a combination of baking soda and water to clean anything that you are unable to remove, such as baked-on residue. Make it work into the grime by scrubbing it with a brush with soft bristles. After removing all of that, you should clean the surface with a cloth.

6. Utilize a cloth that has been dampened with soapy water and then wipe down the exterior of the appliance. Use a fresh damp cloth to remove it completely.

7. After cleaning each component, let it dry completely. After they have been left to dry, you can put together the air fryer.

Chapter 4:
Step-By-Step Air Frying

An air fryer is basically a miniature convection oven: A fan blows heated air over food to cook it quickly. Here are the keys to using it well.

1. If your air fryer is brand new, give it a good cleaning. Take out the basket and the pan, as well as any additional accessories, and wash them thoroughly with soap and water. To clean the exterior as well as the interior of the air fryer, use a paper towel that has been dampened. Clean and dry each of the components, and become familiar with the instructions before continuing.

2. Make sure your food is ready. To ensure that the food cooks evenly, cut it into pieces of a similar size. Make sure you give yourself plenty of time if you want to marinate food. (The majority of foods only need to marinate for a few minutes, but if you want a really robust flavor, you may want to marinate them in the refrigerator for an entire day.) After that, you should pat the pieces dry. Any liquid that is left over on foods will drip into the pan, which could cause the appliance to start smoking.

3. Preheat if it's required. Some models of air fryers need to be preheated before use, while others do not. Learn how to use your appliance by reading the manual that came with it.

4. If you are going to sprinkle crumbs over food, make sure that the coating is firmly pressed onto the food before you sprinkle the crumbs over it. Cooking spray or oil sprayed through a mister can be used to lightly coat other foods. The food should then be placed in the baking pan or the basket.

5. If you are going to be using a pan, make sure that you use the size that is specified in the instruction manual. The majority of air fryers have a pan that measures 6 by 6 by 2 inches, and that is the size for which the recipes in this book were developed. Spray the pan with cooking spray that prevents food from sticking, or line it with parchment paper liners that come with tabs to make it easier to remove food. You could also use a metal bowl that is 6 inches in diameter as long as it easily fits inside the basket and leaves enough space on the top. To safely remove the pan or bowl from the heat, you should use tongs that have a spring-loaded mechanism.

6. Position the basket inside the air fryer and begin setting the timer. Be careful not to cram too much food into the basket. You should give the food a good shake about halfway through the cooking time if you are preparing it in a small quantity, such as tater tots or chopped vegetables. Take out the basket while keeping it attached to the pan, and give it a light shake to redistribute the food. There are some recipes that require you to turn the food. In this step, you should never use your fingers; instead, you should make use of tongs or a large fork.

7. When the food is ready, remove the pan (if it was used) from the basket (if it was used), and then use tongs to remove the food from the basket. Never tip the basket into a dish while it still has the pan attached to it; this will cause any liquids or grease in the pan to spill onto the food, which can cause your fingers to become severely burned.

Chapter 5:

Breakfast Recipes

1.   Spinach and Cheese Breakfast Tart

Prep & Cook: 35mins

Servings: 3-4

Ingredients:

- 3 huge eggs
- 1 1/2 Mugs fresh spinach leaves
- 1/3 Mug heavy cream
- 2 tablespoonful honey Dijon mustard
- 1/2 Mug shredded Gruyere or Monterey Jack cheese
- 1/2 teaspoonful dried thyme

- Seasonings
- Freshly ground black pepper
- Nonstick cooking spray with flour

Directions:

1. Warm up your oven to 320°F (160°C).
2. Whisk the eggs in a mixing bowl until well combined. Combine the heavy cream, spinach, honey Dijon mustard, dried thyme, sea salt, shredded cheese, and freshly ground black pepper in a mixing bowl.
3. Grease a baking dish lightly with nonstick cooking spray and flour.
4. Place the eggs in the dish and bake for 18 to 22 minutes, or until the tart rises and turns golden.
5. Allow the tart to cool for a few minutes before cutting it into wedges. Prepare and enjoy!

2. Bacon and Herb Egg Mugs

Prep & Cook: 40mins

Servings: 6

Ingredients

- 6 huge eggs, lightly beaten
- 1 tablespoonful freshly chopped parsley
- ¼ teaspoonful dry mustard powder
- ¼ Mug unsweetened coconut milk
- 2 tablespoonful finely chopped chives
- 4 cooked bacon strips, crumbled.
- Seasoning of your choice

Directions

1. Spray a muffin tin with cooking spray and preheat the rotisserie to 375°F (190°C).
2. In a mixing bowl, combine the beaten eggs, coconut milk, dry mustard powder, chopped chives, and a little salt and pepper.
3. Gently fold in the crumbled bacon and freshly chopped parsley.
4. Fill the muffin tin halfway with the egg mixture.
5. Bake for 20-25 minutes, or until the egg Mugs are set and slightly golden.
6. Take off from the oven and let cool for a few mins before serving.

3. Creamy Mushroom and Cheese Frittata

Prep & Cook: 25mins

Servings: 4-6

Ingredients:

- 8 huge eggs
- 1/2 Mug heavy cream
- Seasoning of your choice
- 2 Mugs chopped mushrooms
- 1 medium-size red onion, finely chopped
- ½ Mug diced tomatoes
- 1 Mug shredded mozzarella cheese
- 2 teaspoonfuls freshly chopped parsley

Directions:

1. Preheat the air fryer to 330 degrees Fahrenheit (165 degrees Celsius). Cooking Spray an air fryer-safe baking dish with cooking spray.

2. In a mixing bowl, combine the eggs, heavy cream, salt, and black pepper.

3. Add the shredded mozzarella cheese, diced tomatoes, diced red onion, and sliced mushrooms to the beaten eggs. Combine all of the ingredients in a mixing bowl.

4. Place the mixture in the preheated air fryer in the prepared baking dish.

5. Cook the frittata for 8 minutes, or until it is fully cooked and set.

6. When finished, cut the frittata into wedges, and serve with freshly chopped parsley.

4. Cheesy Sausage and Pepper Breakfast Bake

Prep & Cook: 35mins

Servings: 6

Ingredients:

- 1 pound ground breakfast sausage
- 6 huge eggs
- red-bell pepper
- green-bell pepper
- yellow-bell pepper
- 1 sweet onion finely chopped.
- 2 Mugs shredded sharp cheddar cheese.
- Seasoning of your choice
- 2 tablespoonful freshly chopped parsley

Directions:

1. In a skillet over medium heat, brown the ground sausage. Drain any extra fat, then set it aside.

2. Set the air fryer's thermostat to 360°F (180°C).

3. Layer the cooked sausage on the bottom of a casserole dish that can be used in an air fryer.

4. The diced peppers, onion, and cheddar cheese are placed on top of the sausage.

5. In a mixing bowl, combine the eggs, salt, and black pepper. Spread the egg mixture evenly over the casserole's contents.

6. When the eggs are set, place the casserole dish in the hot air fryer for 15 minutes.

7. When finished, sprinkle with freshly chopped parsley and serve hot.

5. Kale and Cottage Cheese Omelet

Prep & Cook: 20mins

Servings: 3

Ingredients:

- 5 huge eggs
- 3 tablespoonful cottage cheese
- 1 Mug chopped kale
- 1/2 tablespoon chopped basil
- Half tablespoon fresh chives, chopped
- Seasoning of your choice

Directions:

1. Add eggs, salt, and black pepper to a bowl and mix well.

2. Cottage cheese, chopped kale, basil, and chives to egg mixture. Gently mix all ingredients.

3. Pour egg mixture into a lightly oiled baking pan.
4. Start the air fryer at 330°F (165°C). Bake the egg mixture in the air fryer for 10 minutes until the omelet is set and light golden.
5. Once cooked, take off from the air-fryer, slice into portions, and serve.

6. Silken Tofu Morning Treat

Prep & Cook :20mins

Servings: 2

Ingredients:

- 1/2 teaspoonful sesame oil
- 1/2 teaspoonful salad-oil
- 8 ounces silken tofu, sliced
- 3 huge eggs
- 2 teaspoonful fish sauce
- Freshly ground black pepper
- 1 teaspoonful cornstarch
- 2 teaspoonful waters

Directions:

1. Your air fryer should be preheated to 390°F (200°C) for 4-5 minutes.
2. The air fryer basket should be covered with a thin layer of cooking oil or cooking spray.
3. The basket should be filled with silken tofu slices.
4. A medium bowl should be used to combine the cornstarch and water. Whisk the mixture until smooth.

5. In a different, larger container, mix the eggs, fish sauce, sesame oil, salad oil, and a small amount of freshly ground black pepper.
6. Pour the egg mixture over the tofu in the air fryer basket.
7. Place the basket in the air-fryer and cook for approximately 10 mins until the tofu is heated and the egg is set.
8. Carefully take off the basket from the air-fryer and serve the tofu treat warm.

7. Spinach and Parmesan Morning Delight

Prep & Cook: 25mins

Servings: 2

Ingredients:

- 1 Mug fresh spinach leaves, washed
- 2 tablespoonful freshly grated Parmesan cheese
- Seasoning of your choice
- 1 tablespoonful white vinegar
- 2 eggs

Directions:

1. To wilt the spinach, steam it or microwave it briefly.
2. To the wilted spinach, season with grated Parmesan cheese, sea salt, and freshly ground black pepper to taste.
3. Arrange the seasoned spinach on serving plates.
4. Fill a pan with water and add white vinegar. Heat the water over low heat until small bubbles form.
5. Carefully crack an egg into a medium size vessel and gently slide it into the simmering water. Repeat with the second egg.

6. Eggs should be poached for three to four minutes for runny yolks and set whites.
7. The poached eggs should be removed using a slotted spoon and served on the spinach.
8. Serve the Florentine eggs warm.

8. Creamy Vanilla French Toast

Prep & Cook: 20mins

Servings: 2

Ingredients:

- 1 huge egg
- 4 slices bread
- 1 teaspoonful vanilla extract
- 2 tablespoonful milk
- 1 tablespoon granulated sweetener
- 2 teaspoonfuls butter

Directions:

1. Whisk the egg in a mixing bowl until well combined.
2. Mash the butter with the back of a spoon until smooth, then stir in the vanilla.
3. Whisk in the milk and granulated sweetener until the sweetener is dissolved.
4. The butter mixture should be applied to both sides of the bread slices using a pastry brush.
5. Bread should be thoroughly saturated in the egg and milk mixture.
6. the air fryer to 400°F (200°C) of temperature.
7. In the air fryer, toast the bread slices for two minutes on one side.

8. Flip the bread slices and continue toasting for an additional 3 mins on the other side.

9. Once the toasts are golden and crispy, cut them into triangles and serve.

9. Paprika Egg Souffle

Prep & Cook: 12mins

Servings: 2

Ingredients:

- 3 huge eggs
- 2 tablespoonful heavy cream
- Seasoning of your choice
- ¼ teaspoonful paprika
- ¼ teaspoonful ground turmeric

Directions:

1. Warm up your air-fryer to 360°Fer (180°C).
2. Separate the eggs and mix them together in a bowl.
3. Stir in the heavy cream to create a creamy texture.
4. Season the egg mixture with a pinch of salt, paprika, and ground turmeric. Mix until evenly distributed.
5. Divide the egg mixture evenly between two ramekins.
6. The egg soufflés should be puffed and set after about 10 minutes of cooking in the air fryer basket with the ramekins inside.
7. The soufflés should be removed from the air fryer and given some time to cool.
8. Serve the paprika egg soufflés for a delightful breakfast treat.

Prep & Cook: 35mins

Servings: 5-6

Ingredients:

- ½ cabbage, finely chopped
- 2-3 leeks cleaned and chopped.
- 2 tablespoonful coconut oil
- 3-4 celery ribs, diced.
- bell-pepper, diced.
- carrots, diced.
- Two garlic cloves, minced.
- Four Mugs vegetable broth
- teaspoonful Italian and creole seasoning
- Freshly ground black pepper, to taste
- 2-3 Mugs mixed salad greens

Directions:

1. Warm up the air-fryer on the sauté setting and warm up the coconut oil.
2. Add the chopped vegetables one by one, starting with carrots, and stir well after each addition.
3. Reserve the minced garlic for the end to prevent bitterness.
4. Season the mixture with Creole seasoning, Italian seasoning, and freshly ground-black-pepper.
5. Add the vegetable broth and set the air-fryer to the soup setting. Cook for 20 mins with the vent closed.
6. After cooking, take off the lid and open the vent to release steam.

7. Add the mixed salad greens to the soup and stir until wilted.
8. Taste and adjust the seasoning if needed before serving.

11. Egg and Ham Mugs

Prep & Cook: 15mins

Servings: 2

Ingredients:

- 4 huge eggs
- 4 slices deli ham
- 1/2 Mug shredded medium Cheddar cheese.
- 1/4 Mug diced green-bell-pepper.
- 2 tablespoonsful diced red-bell.
- 2 tablespoonsful diced white onion.
- 2 tablespoonful full-fat sour cream

Directions:

1. Line four muffin Mugs with a slice of deli ham each.
2. In a huge vessel, whisk together eggs and sour cream until combined. Add diced green pepper, red pepper, and onion. Stir well.
3. Transfer the egg mixture into the ham-lined muffin Mugs. Sprinkle shredded Cheddar cheese on top.
4. Place muffin mugs in the air fryer basket. Set a timer for 12 minutes, or until the tops are golden and the eggs are set and preheat the oven to 320°F (160°C).
5. Once cooked, take off the Mugs from the air-fryer and serve hot.

Prep & Cook: 20 mins

Servings: 4

Ingredients:

- Crescent rolls, chilled (9.2 oz.) package
- 1 tablespoon ground cinnamon
- 2 oz. raisins
- 1/3 Mug butter
- 2 tablespoonful granulated sweetener
- 1/3 Mug chopped pecans.
- Cooking spray (salad-oil)
- 2 tablespoonful maple syrup
- 1/3 Mug brown sweetener

Directions:

1. Warm up the air-fryer to 345°F (175°C).
2. In a small pot, melt the butter and mix in maple syrup and brown sweetener until well combined.
3. Lightly spray an 8-inch baking pan with salad-oil.
4. Sprinkle granulated sweetener, raisins, and chopped pecans in the pan.
5. Unroll the crescent rolls onto a cutting board. Sprinkle the rolls with ground cinnamon and gently press it in.
6. Roll the dough back up and cut it into eight pieces.
7. Dip each roll into the butter mixture, then place them in the prepared baking pan.

8. For 8 to 10 minutes, or until golden and thoroughly cooked, bake the rolls in the baking pan inside the air fryer basket.

9. After removing the rolls from the air fryer, immediately top them with the remaining butter mixture.

10. Serve the cinnamon roll delights warm.

13. Loaded Disco Fries

Prep & Cook: 40 mins

Servings: 4

Ingredients:

- 4.40 grams of cream cheese
- 1/3 Mug shredded mozzarella cheese
- Mug shredded Cheddar cheese
- Two jalapeños, finely chopped.
- 1/2 Mug bread crumbs
- 2 huge eggs
- 1/2 Mug all-purpose flour
- Seasoning of your choice
- Cooking oil

Directions:

1. Heat your air-fryer to 380°F (190°C).
2. Stir cream cheese, mozzarella, Cheddar, and chopped jalapenos in a medium bowl until smooth.
3. On a baking sheet, shape the cheese mixture into golf-ball-sized spheres. For best results, freeze the balls for 15 minutes.

40

4. Spray oil into the air fryer basket.

5. Each flour, beaten egg, and breadcrumbs need a shallow bowl.

6. Remove the cheese balls from the freezer and coat them in flour, egg, and breadcrumbs.

7. Place the coated cheese balls in the air-fryer basket without touching.

8. Spray the coated cheese balls with a light layer of cooking oil.

9. Air fry the cheese bites at 350°F (175°C) for about 8-10 mins, until they are golden and crispy.

10. Allow the jalapeño cheese bites to cool slightly before serving.

14. Jalapeno Cheese Balls

Prep & Cook: 30mins

Servings: 12

Ingredients:

- 1 (28-ounce) bag frozen steak fries
- Cooking oil spray
- Salt
- Pepper
- 1/2 Mug beef gravy
- 1 Mug shredded mozzarella cheese
- 2 scallions, green parts only, chopped

Directions:

1. Fire up your air-fryer at 400°F (200°C).
2. Air-fry frozen steak fries for 10 minutes.

3. Open the air-fryer and shake the basket for even cooking. Sprinkle salt and pepper on fries and oil them. Cook another 8 minutes.
4. Heat beef gravy in a microwave-safe dish for 30 seconds.
5. After cooking the fries, sprinkle them with mozzarella cheese and air fry for 2 minutes until melted and bubbly.
6. The fries can be placed on a platter after air-frying.
7. Pour warm beef gravy over loaded fries and top with chopped scallions.
8. Hot and gooey loaded fries should be served.

15. Buffalo Cauliflower Bites

Prep & Cook: 40mins

Servings: 4

Ingredients:

- Mug all-purpose flour.
- Mug of water
- 1 teaspoonful garlic powder
- 1 huge head cauliflower, cut into florets (4 Mugs)
- Cooking oil spray
- 1/3 Mug buffalo wing sauce

Directions:

1. The air fryer should be heated to 370°F (188°C).
2. In a large bowl, whisk together the flour, water, and garlic powder until the mixture resembles pancake batter.
3. Cauliflower florets should be added to the batter and coated evenly.
4. Spray cooking oil on the air fryer basket to avoid sticking.

5. With care to avoid crowding the air fryer, put the coated cauliflower florets inside. Whenever necessary, cook in batches.

6. Cauliflower should be cooked for 6 minutes, with the basket being shaken halfway through to ensure even cooking.

7. The cauliflower should be taken out of the air fryer and placed in a very large container.

8. Give the cauliflower a thorough coating of buffalo wing sauce.

9. Back in the air fryer, fry the coated cauliflower for an additional 6 minutes, or until golden and crispy.

10. Allow the buffalo cauliflower bites to cool slightly before serving.

16. Healthy Cheese Pockets

Prep & Cook: 8 hrs. 15mins

Servings: 6

Ingredients:

For the Dough:
- 3/4 Mug Almond Flour
- 1/2 Mug Coconut Oil
- 1/2 teaspoonful Salt

For the Filling:
- 1/2 Mug Raw Cashews, soaked overnight
- 1 tablespoonful Nutritional Yeast
- 1/2 teaspoonful Garlic Powder
- 1/4 teaspoonful Salt

Directions:

1. Almond flour, coconut oil, and salt should be mixed together to form a dough. Use your hands to thoroughly combine everything and distribute it evenly.
2. Soak the cashews, then blend them in a food processor with the nutritional yeast, garlic powder, and salt until smooth.
3. Roll the dough into an 8-by-12-inch rectangle on an almond flour-dusted surface.
4. Make six squares out of the dough.
5. Fill each square with a spoonful of cashew filling.
6. Make triangles out of the dough and seal the edges.
7. Preheat the air fryer to 380°F (193°C).
8. The air fryer basket should be sprayed with nonstick cooking spray.
9. Cook the cheese pockets for 15 minutes, or until they are golden and crispy.
10. Serve the nutty almond cheese pockets warm.

17. Chinese Orange Tofu

Prep & Cook: 40 mins

Servings: 4

Ingredients:

- Pound extra-firm tofu, drained and pressed.
- 1 tablespoonful tamari
- 1 tablespoonful cornstarch (or arrowroot powder)
- Zest of 1 orange
- 1/3 Mug orange juice
- 1/2 Mug water
- 2 teaspoonfuls cornstarch (or arrowroot powder)

- 1/4 teaspoonful crushed red pepper flakes.
- teaspoonful fresh ginger
- teaspoonful fresh garlic
- 1 tablespoon pure maple syrup

Directions:

1. Cut the tofu into cubes and marinate in tamari for 15 mins.
2. Toss the marinated tofu cubes in cornstarch until coated.
3. Warm up the air-fryer to 390°F (199°C).
4. Shake the air fryer basket occasionally during the 10-minute cooking time and place the coated tofu inside.
5. Orange zest, orange juice, water, cornstarch, red pepper flakes, ginger, garlic, and maple syrup are whisked together in a bowl.
6. Transfer the orange sauce over the cooked tofu in the air-fryer basket.
7. To ensure that the tofu is evenly coated with sauce, cook it for an additional 10 minutes while shaking the basket occasionally.
8. Toss the orange tofu with rice and some steamed vegetables for a delicious meal.

18. Asparagus Phyllo Bundles

Prep & Cook: 24 mins

Servings:4

Ingredients:

- 4 tablespoonful minced onion
- 3 garlic cloves, minced.
- 3 tablespoonful grated carrot

- 2 teaspoonful salad-oil
- 4 tablespoonful frozen baby peas, thawed.
- 3 tablespoons of room temperature nonfat cream cheese
- 8 sheets of thawed frozen phyllo dough.
- Salad-oil spray

Directions:

1. Start the air-fryer at 350°F (175°C).
2. Cook onion, garlic, carrot, and salad-oil in a skillet over medium heat until tender. Stir in thawed baby peas. Cool place.
3. Combine sautéed vegetables with nonfat cream cheese.
4. Spray phyllo dough with salad-oil spray. Place remaining phyllo sheets on top of each other.
5. Split the layered phyllo sheets into four equal strips.
6. Put a spoonful of vegetable-cream cheese mixture at the bottom of each strip. Continue folding the phyllo over the mixture to form a triangle until the end.
7. Seam-side down, place phyllo bundles in air-fryer basket. Dress the bundles with salad oil.
8. Air fry phyllo bundles for 4-7 minutes until golden brown and crispy.
9. Serve the vegetable phyllo bundles warm.

19. Split Pea and Ham Soup

Prep & Cook: 55mins

Servings: 4-6

Ingredients:

- 3 tablespoonful ghee

- 4-pounds asparagus, cut into 2-inch pieces
- 1 white onion, diced
- 4 Mugs chicken broth
- 1/2 teaspoonful thyme
- 1 ham bone
- 5 cloves garlic, pressed
- 1 teaspoonful ground cumin
- 2 teaspoonfuls balsamic vinegar
- 1 teaspoonful chopped basil
- Seasoning of your choice

Directions:

1. Set the air-fryer to sauté mode and melt the ghee.
2. Add diced onion to the air-fryer and sauté until browned, about 5 mins.
3. Place ham bone, pressed garlic, chicken broth, and asparagus into the air-fryer. Allow it to simmer for about 5 mins.
4. Add thyme, ground cumin, balsamic vinegar, chopped basil, salt, and black pepper to the mixture. Stir well.
5. Adjust the air-fryer to high pressure and set the timer for 45 mins.
6. Once the cooking is complete, carefully take off the ham bone and discard it.
7. The soup may be blended smooth using an immersion blender.
8. Serve the split pea and ham soup in vessels, and enjoy the rich flavors.

Prep & Cook: 15 mins

Servings: 3

Ingredients:

- 1 extra-firm tofu block (about 18 ounces)
- 2 tablespoonful low-sodium soy sauce
- tablespoon ketchup
- tbsp honey
- 1 Mug store-bought barbecue sauce, divided

Directions:

1. Drain and press the tofu to take off excess moisture. Cut it into bite-sized pieces.
2. Whisk together the honey, ketchup, and soy sauce in a separate container.
3. Tofu should be marinated in the mixture for approximately ten minutes.
4. the air fryer to 400 degrees Fahrenheit before using it (200 degrees Celsius).
5. Arrange in a single layer one-half of the tofu that has been marinated in the basket of the air fryer.
6. Tofu should be cooked for ten minutes, turning it over once halfway through.
7. After it has finished cooking, remove the tofu and place it in a container.
8. After the tofu has been cooked, pour half a mug's worth of barbecue sauce over it and toss to coat.
9. Return the sauced tofu to the air fryer's basket and cook it for an additional five minutes.
10. After they have finished cooking, the smoky barbecue tofu bites should be served with the remaining barbecue sauce for dipping.

Chapter 6:
Lunch Recipes

21. Indonesian Chicken Drumettes

Prep & Cook: 52 mins

Servings: 4

Ingredients:

- 1½ lbs. chicken wing drumettes
- Cooking oil spray
- tbsp low-sodium soy sauce
- ½ tsp cornstarch
- tsp finely minced shallot
- ½ tsp finely minced fresh turmeric

- tsp chili garlic sauce
- sea salt
- 1 tsps. fresh lemon zest
- 2 tsps. agave nectar
- 2 tbsp fresh cilantro, chopped.

Directions:

1. Begin by patting dry the chicken drumettes using paper towels. Lightly coat with cooking oil spray.
2. Set the temperature of your air fryer to 400 degrees (200 degrees Celsius).
3. The drumettes should be arranged in a single layer in the air fryer's basket.
4. Cooking time for drumettes is 22 minutes, during which time the basket needs to be shaken twice.
5. Remove the drumettes from the air fryer once they have achieved the desired level of crispiness.
6. Stir the soy sauce and cornstarch together until smooth in a small pot while the drumettes are cooking.
7. The additions that need to be made are shallot, turmeric, chili garlic sauce, salt, lemon zest, and agave nectar.
8. Place the saucepan on the stovetop over medium heat, and while stirring the liquid frequently, continue to do so until it begins to thicken and boil.
9. After the drumsticks have been cooked, they should be thrown into a large mixing bowl.
10. Carefully toss the drumettes with the sauce that has been prepared.
11. Just before serving, top the dish with finely chopped fresh cilantro.

Prep & Cook: 54 mins

Servings: 3

Ingredients:

- 500 g duck breast fillets, thinly sliced
- 200 g baby bok choy, chopped
- 200 g broccoli florets
- 12 shiitake mushrooms, sliced
- 3 spring onions, diagonally sliced
- cloves garlic, minced
- Three red chili peppers, thinly sliced
- ½ red bell pepper, cut into strips
- 4 cm fresh galangal, thinly sliced
- Juice of 1 lime
- 100 ml vegetable broth
- Low-sodium soy sauce, 6 tablespoons
- 1 tablespoon of sesame oil, roasted
- 1 tsp agave syrup
- Himalayan pink salt
- Freshly ground black pepper

Directions:

1. Begin by thinly slicing the duck breast fillets.
2. Chop the baby bok choy and separate the broccoli florets from the stalk.
3. Cut the shiitake mushrooms into slices and the spring onions into thin, diagonal slices.

4. Sesame oil should be heated in a big pan over medium heat to brown the duck. Take out of the equation.
5. In the same pan, stir-fry the broccoli and red bell pepper for a short while.
6. Stir-fry the mushrooms, garlic, and galangal after adding them.
7. Add the red peppers and baby bok choy.
8. Return the cooked duck to the pan after adding the vegetable broth.
9. Squeeze in the lime juice and drizzle with soy sauce and agave syrup.
10. Himalayan salt and freshly ground black pepper should be used to season.
11. Once the flavors have melded, cook for a few more minutes.
12. Sliced spring onions are a nice garnish for the pan-seared duck.

23. Curry Turkey Samosas

Prep & Cook: 22 mins

Servings: 2

Ingredients:

- 2 oz shredded cooked turkey meat
- tsp ground cumin
- ground coriander
- tsp mild curry powder
- Seasoning of your choice
- Coconut milk, for moistening
- 1 small egg, whisked
- 2 puff pastry sheets

Directions:

1. Combine the shredded turkey with the cumin, coriander, curry powder, salt, and pepper in a mixing bowl.
2. Add a splash of coconut milk to create a moist mixture.
3. Lay out the puff pastry sheets and place the turkey mixture onto one half of each sheet.
4. Fold the pastry over to create pocket shapes resembling samosas.
5. Brush the folded pockets with the whisked egg for a golden finish.
6. Warm up your rotisserie to 375°F (190°C) and bake the pockets for about 15 mins until golden.
7. Serve the spiced turkey pockets warm.

24. Chicken Tikka Kebab

Prep & Cook: 28 mins

Servings: 4

Ingredients:

- lb boneless, skinless chicken thighs, cubed
- tbsp salad-oil
- ½ Mug red onion, chopped
- ½ Mug green bell pepper, chopped
- ½ Mug yellow bell pepper, chopped
- Wedge of lime for presentation
- Fresh cilantro leaves, for garnish

For marinade:
- ½ Mug Greek yogurt
- tablespoonful of minced fresh ginger
- tablespoonful of minced fresh garlic
- tbsp lime juice

- tsp paprika
- ½ tsp ground turmeric
- ground cumin
- ground coriander
- ½ tsp dried fenugreek leaves
- Salt, to taste

Directions:

1. In a mixing bowl, stir all the marinade's components until thoroughly blended.
2. After cutting the chicken into cubes and adding it to the marinade, it should marinate for at least 30 minutes.
3. Skewer the marinated chicken and vegetables, alternating between the two.
4. Get your grill or grill pan nice and toasty.
5. Grill the skewers for 10 to 12 minutes, flipping them regularly and brushing with salad oil, until they are fully cooked and have a faint sear.
6. Garnish with lime wedges and fresh cilantro leaves.
7. Serve the grilled chicken tikka skewers with your favorite dipping sauce.

25. Tequila Orange Chicken

Prep & Cook: 1hr 20mins

Servings: 4

Ingredients:

- ¼ Mug tequila
- 2 shallots, finely minced
- 1/3 Mug fresh orange juice
- 3 tbsp brown sweetener

- 3 tbsp wildflower honey
- 3 tbsp whole coriander seeds
- 4 garlic cloves, minced
- 4 lbs bone-in chicken thighs Salt and freshly ground black pepper.

Directions:

1. In a vessel, combine tequila, minced shallot, orange juice, brown sweetener, honey, coriander seeds, and minced garlic.
2. Seal the package of chicken thighs with the marinade inside. Put the bag in the fridge for at least two hours with the seal tight.
3. Air fryer temperature should be set at 390 degrees Fahrenheit (200 degrees Celsius).
4. Prepare food in an air-fryer by adding a grill pan.
5. Place the marinated chicken on the grill pan and cook for 40 minutes, flipping every 10 minutes to ensure even cooking.
6. While the chicken cooks, transfer the marinade to a saucepan and heat until thickened.
7. Before serving, basting the chicken with the reduced marinade is a nice touch.

26. Turkey Slice in Creamy White Wine Sauce

Prep & Cook: 1 hr. 30mins

Servings: 3

Ingredients:

- 1 lb turkey fillets, thinly sliced
- 1 package cream
- 1 can sliced mushrooms

- 3 onions, thinly sliced
- 1 glass white wine
- Salad-oil
- Lemon juice
- Black pepper
- Salt

Directions:

1. Marinate the turkey fillets in lemon juice for one hour, then season them with salt and black pepper.
2. The onions should be cooked in the salad oil until they are a light golden color. Eliminate and set aside.
3. In the same skillet, cook the turkey fillets for 30 minutes at 400 degrees Fahrenheit (200 degrees Celsius) in the air fryer.
4. Add the sliced mushrooms and white wine to the skillet and cover.
5. Once the turkey is cooked, place the sautéed onions back into the skillet.
6. Add the cream, raise the heat, and season it.
7. Serve the creamy lemon turkey over the fillets.

27. Short Ribs in Soy-Pear Sauce

Prep & Cook: 50 mins

Servings: 4

Ingredients:

- 2 green onions, chopped
- tsp vegetable oil
- Three garlic cloves, minced

- 3 slices of fresh ginger
- 4 lbs beef short ribs
- ½ Mug water
- ½ Mug low-sodium soy sauce
- ¼ Mug rice wine
- ¼ Mug pear juice
- 2 tsp sesame oil

Directions:

1. Green onions, ginger, and garlic should all be sautéed in vegetable oil for one minute over medium heat.
2. In the skillet, put the beef short ribs, water, soy sauce, rice wine, sesame oil, and pear juice. Mix thoroughly.
3. Place the mixture in the air fryer and cook for about 35 minutes at 350°F (175°C).
4. Divide the ribs and sauce onto plates and serve.

28. Creamy and Spicy Pork Gratin

Prep & Cook: 60 mins

Servings: 6

Ingredients:

- Two tbsp salad-oil
- 2 lbs pork tenderloin, sliced
- Seasoning of your choice
- ¼ tsp red chili flakes
- tsp dried thyme

- tablespoonful Mustard with a Dijon flavor
- 1 Mug cottage cheese
- 1 ½ Mugs chicken broth

Directions:

1. Heat your Air-fryer to 350°F (175°C).
2. Pan-sear pork slices in salad-oil over medium-high heat for 6-7 minutes until golden. Take off and wait.
3. Place seared pork slices in a greased casserole dish.
4. Add salt, black pepper, chili flakes, and dry thyme for flavor.
5. Pour Dijon mustard, cottage cheese, and chicken broth into a bowl. Spread the mixture over the meat in the baking dish.
6. Bake the gratin for 15 minutes in the heated air-fryer until bubbly.

29. Tarragon Beef Shanks

Prep & Cook: 1h 40mins

Servings: 2

Ingredients

- 2 tbsp salad-oil
- 2 lbs. beef shank, cubed
- Seasoning of your choice
- finely diced onion
- 2 celery stalks, diced finely
- 1 Mug Marsala wine
- 2 tsp dried tarragon

Directions:

7. Put the beef shank cubes in a bowl and season with salt and pepper.

8. Set the air fryer's temperature to 350°F (175°C).

9. The diced onion and celery should be cooked in a skillet with salad oil until tender. Take out and place aside.

10. Cook the beef shank cubes in the Air-fryer basket for an hour while stirring occasionally.

11. Transfer in the Marsala wine and add the sautéed onion and celery.

12. Stir in dried tarragon.

13. Serve the fragrant tarragon beef stew warm.

30. Beef Taco Fried Egg Rolls

Prep & Cook: 23 mins

Servings: 8

Ingredients:

- tsp chopped fresh cilantro
- 2 garlic cloves, minced
- 1 tbsp salad-oil
- 1 Mug shredded Mexican cheese blend
- ½ packet taco seasoning
- ½ can cilantro lime Rotel (diced tomatoes and green chilies)
- ½ chopped onion
- Wrappers for 16 egg rolls
- 1 lb lean ground beef

Directions:

1. Warm up your Air-fryer to 400°F (200°C).

2. In a skillet, sauté chopped onion, garlic, and ground beef until cooked. Add taco seasoning and cilantro lime Rotel. Mix well.
3. Lay out egg roll wrappers and moisten with water.
4. Fill each wrapper with beef mixture and top with shredded cheese.
5. Fold the wrappers diagonally to seal, using water to secure the edges.
6. Brush salad oil on the folded spring rolls before placing them in the air fryer.
7. Cook until crispy after flipping the food after 8 minutes of air-frying.
8. Garnish with chopped cilantro and serve.

31. Jamaican Meatballs

Prep & Cook: 40 mins

Servings: 4

Ingredients:

- 2 tbsp Jamaican Jerk Dry Rub
- 100g ground chicken
- 100g breadcrumbs
- 4 tbsp raw honey
- 1 tbsp soy sauce

Directions:

1. In a vessel, combine ground chicken, breadcrumbs, and 1 tbsp Jamaican Jerk Dry Rub. Mix well and shape into meatball shapes using a meatball press.
2. Cook the chicken meatballs for 15 minutes in an air fryer at 180 °C (350 °F).
3. In another mixing vessel, mix together soy sauce, raw honey, and the remaining Jamaican Jerk Dry Rub.
4. Once the meatballs are cooked, dip or toss them in the sauce and serve.

Prep & Cook: 26 mins

Servings: 2

Ingredients:

- 2 pork chops
- Seasoning of your choice
- 1 tbsp salad-oil
- 2 tbsp butter
- 1 shallot, sliced
- 1 handful sage, chopped
- tsp lemon juice

Directions:

1. Salt and black pepper pork chops, rub with salad oil, and air-fry. Flip halfway through 10 minutes at 370°F (190°C).
2. Heat butter in a pan on medium. Sauté sliced shallot for 2 minutes. After adding chopped sage and lemon juice and cooking for a few minutes, remove from heat.
3. Plate the pork chops, pour the sage sauce over them, and serve.

Prep & Cook: 40 mins

Servings: 4

Ingredients:

- 4 medium-sized pork chops
- 1 Mug breadcrumbs
- 2 medium-sized eggs
- Pinch of salt and pepper
- ½ tbsp mint (dried and ground or fresh, finely chopped)

Directions:

1. Your air fryer should be heated to 350°F (175°C).
2. In a bowl, the eggs must be thoroughly combined before being set aside. Toss the breadcrumbs with the mint, salt, and pepper in a separate bowl.
3. Each pork chop should first be covered in egg wash before being breaded and fried. Pork chops that have been covered ought to go in an air fryer basket lined with foil.
4. For 15 minutes, air-fry the pork chops at 350°F (175°C) until they are golden and crispy.
5. Serve the minty chicken-fried pork chops hot.

Prep & Cook: 40 mins

Servings: 4

Ingredients:

- 1.5 lbs pork stew meat, cubed.
- 2 tbsp avocado oil
- Seasoning of your choice
- ½ lb white mushrooms, sliced
- 1 Mug yellow onion, chopped.
- 6 garlic cloves, minced.
- 6 Mugs vegetable stock
- tbsp parsley,

Directions:

1. Heat avocado oil in the sauté setting on your air fryer. For 3–4 minutes, brown the pork stew meat.
2. Put in some onions, mushrooms, garlic, salt, and pepper. Keep cooking for another 2 minutes.
3. Cook for 20 minutes on high with the lid on and some vegetable stock.
4. After allowing the pressure to drop on its own for 10 minutes, the stew is ready to be served in individual bowls and garnished with parsley.

Prep & Cook: 50 mins

Servings: 4

Ingredients:

- 1 Mug rice milk
- 1 tbsp soy sauce
- 1 tbsp red curry paste
- 1 tbsp sweetener
- 8 chicken wings
- 2 tbsp fresh parsley, chopped

Directions:

1. Warm up your air-fryer to 380°F (193°C).
2. In a vessel, mix rice milk, soy sauce, red curry paste, and sweetener. Marinate the chicken wings in this mixture for 20 mins. Grease the air-fryer basket with cooking spray.
3. After marinating, drain the wings and reserve the marinade.
4. The wings should be air-fried for 18-20 minutes and flipped once while cooking.
5. In a saucepan, cook the reserved marinade until it thickens (about 8 mins).
6. Toss the cooked wings in the sauce and sprinkle with chopped parsley before serving.

Prep & Cook: 30 mins

Servings: 4

Ingredients:

- Five bone-in, skin-on chicken thighs
- Two tsp grated ginger
- Juice of 1 lime
- tbsp chili garlic sauce
- 1/4 Mug salad-oil
- 1/3 Mug soy sauce

Directions:

1. Mix grated ginger, lime juice, chili garlic sauce, salad oil, and soy sauce in a large bowl.
2. Marinate chicken thighs in the container. Refrigerate 30 minutes.

3. Start by heating your air fryer to 400°F (200 degrees Celsius).

4. Air fry the chicken thighs for 15-20 minutes, flipping once, until an instant-read thermometer reads 165 degrees Fahrenheit (74 degrees Celsius).

5. Serve the spicy Asian chicken thighs.

37. Easy General Tso's Chicken

Prep & Cook: 29 mins

Servings: 4

Ingredients:

- tbsp sesame oil
- minced garlic
- 1/2 tsp ground ginger
- 1 Mug chicken broth
- 5tbsp soy sauce, divided.
- 1/2 tsp sriracha, plus more for serving.
- 2 tbsp hoisin sauce
- 4 tbsp cornstarch, divided.
- 4 boneless, skinless chicken breasts, cut into 1-inch pieces.
- Salad-oil spray
- 2 medium scallions, sliced (green parts only)
- Sesame seeds, for garnish

Directions:

1. Warm garlic, ginger, and sesame oil in a small saucepan over low heat. Hold 1 minute.

2. Add chicken stock, 2 tablespoons soy sauce, hot sauce, and hoisin. Blend with a whisk. After 5 minutes, add 2 tablespoons of cornstarch and cook until thickened. Turn off and store stove.

3. Preheat the air fryer to 375 degrees Fahrenheit (190 degrees Celsius).

4. In a bowl, combine the remaining two tablespoons of soy sauce with the cornstarch, and then toss the chicken in the mixture.

5. Put the chicken pieces in the air fryer basket so that they don't touch each other. After ten minutes in the air fryer, give the food one turn.

6. When the chicken is done cooking, add it to the sauce you've made.

7. Serve the General Tso's chicken with scallions, sesame seeds, and additional sriracha if desired.

38. Warm Chicken and Spinach Salad

Prep & Cook: 46 mins

Servings: 5

Ingredients:

- 3 (5-ounce) boneless, skinless chicken breasts, cubed
- 5 tsp extra-virgin salad-oil
- 1/2 milligram of dried thyme
- a small zucchini that has been cut into strips, a medium red onion, and sliced red bell pepper are all included.
- 3 tablespoons of lemon juice that has been freshly squeezed.
- 6 ounces of baby spinach leaves that are fresh.

Directions:

1. To begin, set your air fryer's temperature to 375 degrees Fahrenheit and let it preheat (190 degrees Celsius).

2. In a large bowl, cut the chicken into cubes and add the thyme as well as the salad oil. Toss your coat.

3. To use an air fryer, transfer the chicken mixture to a medium metal bowl that can fit into the basket.

4. Fry in an air fryer for 20 minutes at 375 degrees Fahrenheit (190 degrees Celsius), stirring once.

5. Put in some red bell pepper, zucchini, and sliced onion. Keep air frying for an additional 5-6 minutes, or until the vegetables are tender.

6. Add freshly squeezed lemon juice once cooked.

7. Place the baby spinach leaves in a serving dish. Toss the warm chicken and vegetable mixture on top and serve.

39. Quail in White Wine Sauce

Prep & Cook: 12 hrs. 90min

Servings: 4

Ingredients:

- 4 huge quail
- 1 bottle of dry white wine
  tsp sweet paprika
- tsp hot paprika
- 1/2 package fresh sage, chopped or 2 tbsp dehydrated sage
- 1 head minced garlic
- 1/4 tsp virgin salad-oil
- 1.7 oz. butter
- Salt to taste

- 4 rosemary sprigs

Directions:

1. Wash the quail thoroughly and pat them dry. Boil salted water in a skillet to cover the quail. Once boiling, place the quail in the pan, cover, and cook for 5 mins. Drain and let them cool.
2. Sprinkle a little minced garlic inside each quail. Place the quail in a huge vessel and transfer white wine over them. Add sweet and hot paprika, salad-oil, and sage. Marinate for a minimum of 12 hours in the fridge.
3. Take off the quail from the marinade and place them in a pan with butter.
4. Warm up the air-fryer to about 200°F (93°C) and bake the quail for 90 mins, turning them and sprinkling with the marinade every 15 mins.
5. Serve the quail with rosemary sprigs as garnish.

40. Caribbean Chicken Thighs

Prep & Cook: 40 mins

Servings: 8

Ingredients:

- 3.5 kilograms of chicken thigh fillets that are boneless and skinless
- Black pepper in ground form
- 1 tablespoon of coriander seed, ground
- Salt
- tablespoon of cinnamon powder
- tablespoon of cayenne pepper and 1 and a half teaspoons of ground ginger
- 1 and a half milligrams of ground nutmeg
- Three tablespoons of coconut oil

Directions:

1. Remove chicken from packaging and dry. Salt and ground black pepper both sides. Leave the chicken at room temperature for 30 minutes.
2. In a small vessel, mix ground coriander seed, ground cinnamon, cayenne pepper, ground ginger, and ground nutmeg.
3. The chicken thighs are coated with coconut oil after being thoroughly covered in the spice mixture.
4. Without crowding, place four pieces of chicken in the air fryer basket. Ten minutes in the oven or air fryer at 390°F (200°C).
5. The chicken must be taken out of the basket and put in an oven-safe dish with the foil tightly covering it to keep it warm during baking.
6. Repeat the process of air-frying to finish cooking the remaining chicken.

Chapter 7:
Dinner Recipes

41. Orange Turkey Burgers

Prep & Cook: 30 mins

Servings: 5

Ingredients:

- 1.5-pound Ground Turkey
- teaspoonful Ground Mustard Seed
- tablespoon Grape Nuts Nuggets
- 1/4 teaspoonful Chinese Five Spice
- 1 Diced Scallion

Orange Basting Sauce:

- 1/2 Mug Orange Marmalade
- tablespoon Soy Sauce
- 1 teaspoonful Fish Sauce
- 2 teaspoonfulfuls Oyster Sauce

Orange Aioli:

- tablespoon Orange Juice
- teaspoonful Orange Zest
- 1/2 Mug Mayonnaise
- 1 teaspoonful Ground Chili Paste

Directions:

1. Before chilling the bowl in the refrigerator, combine all the ingredients for the Orange Aioli in a small bowl.
2. The Orange Basting Sauce may be made in a separate dish by combining the necessary ingredients.
3. At 200°C (390°F), the air fryer should be preheated for approximately 10 minutes.
4. In a medium vessel, combine the ground turkey, ground mustard seed, Grape Nuts Nuggets, Chinese Five Spice, diced scallion, and 1 tablespoon of the Orange Basting Sauce.
5. Make six patties from the mixture, with a well indented in the middle of each.
6. Before putting the patties inside the air-fryer basket, lightly coat the interior of the basket with cooking oil.
7. The burgers should be cooked for nine minutes at a temperature of 180 degrees Celsius (350 degrees Fahrenheit), with flipping occurring every four minutes on average.
8. Baste the burgers with the Orange Basting Sauce every 2 mins while cooking.

9. After the initial 9 mins of cooking, baste the burgers again and cook for an additional 3 mins.
10. Serve the hot turkey burgers along with the Orange Aioli.

42. Healthy Turkey Lettuce Wraps

Prep & Cook: 27 mins

Servings: 4

Ingredients

- 250g Ground Turkey
- Small Onion, finely chopped
- Garlic Clove, minced
- 2 tablespoonful Extra Virgin Salad-oil
- Head of Lettuce
- teaspoonful Cumin
- 1/2 tablespoon Fresh Ginger, sliced
- 2 tablespoonful Apple Cider Vinegar
- 2 tablespoonful Freshly Chopped Cilantro
- teaspoonful Freshly Ground Black Pepper
- teaspoonful Sea Salt

Directions

1. Sauté the minced garlic and chopped onion in extra virgin salad oil at 350 degrees Fahrenheit until fragrant and translucent.
2. Add the ground turkey and cook for 5-8 mins or until done to your desired level.

3. Mix in the cumin, sliced ginger, apple cider vinegar, freshly chopped cilantro, black pepper, and sea salt. Continue cooking for an additional 5 mins.

4. Wrap a lettuce leaf around a spoonful of the turkey filling and serve. Eat up that turkey lettuce wrap with pride.

43. Spiced Veggie Burger

Prep & Cook: 45 mins

Servings: 6

Ingredients:

- 1/4 Mug Desiccated Coconut
- 1/2 Mug Oats
- 1/2-pound Cauliflower, steamed and diced
- 1 Mug Breadcrumbs
- Flax Egg (1 tablespoon Flaxseed Meal + 3 tablespoonful Water)
- 1 teaspoonful Mustard Powder
- teaspoonfuls Chives
- teaspoonfuls Melted Coconut Oil
- tsps. Minced Garlic
- 2 teaspoonfuls Parsley
- 2 teaspoonfuls Thyme
- Three tablespoonful Plain Flour
- Salt and Pepper, to taste

Directions:

1. Warm up the air-fryer to 390°F (200°C).

2. Mix together desiccated coconut, oats, cauliflower, breadcrumbs, flax egg, mustard powder, chives, melted coconut oil, chopped garlic, parsley, thyme, plain flour, salt, and pepper in a large mixing bowl. Coat everything with a thick layer of mixing.
3. Make 8 burger patties out of the mixture.
4. Coat the patties with breadcrumbs and lay them in the air fryer basket without letting them touch.
5. Air fry at 390°F (200°C) for 10 to 15 mins until the patties are crisp.
6. Serve the spiced veggie burgers hot.

44. Pulled BBQ Beef Sandwiches

Prep & Cook: 70 mins

Servings: 6

Ingredients:

- 2 pounds Beef of Choice
- 2 Mugs Water
- 4 Mugs Finely Shredded Cabbage
- 1/2 Mug Your Favorite BBQ Sauce
- 1 Mug Ketchup
- 1/3 Mug Worcestershire Sauce
- 1 tablespoon Horseradish
- 1 tablespoon Mustard
- 6 Buns

Directions:

7. The ingredients should be added to your Instant Crisp Air-fryer and stirred.

8. 35 minutes on high pressure. The "Pressure" button can be used to change the time.

9. Permit a natural release of pressure.

10. Close the air fryer lid after removing the Instant Crisp lid. Choose the AIR-FRY mode, increase the heat to 390°F, and cook for 15 minutes, checking after 10 minutes and increasing the cooking time by 5 minutes if necessary.

11. Set the beef aside. Switch the Instant Crisp Air-fryer to "Sauté" mode and cook the sauce until it reaches the desired consistency.

12. Serve the pulled BBQ beef on buns and enjoy.

45. Vegetable Tuna Melt

Prep & Cook: 26 mins

Servings: 2

Ingredients:

- Four tiny cod fillets (Skin Take off)
- To taste, add pepper and salt.
- 1 teaspoon of flour
- Dried Breadcrumbs, 40g
- 250g Frozen Peas
- Tablespoon Creme Fraiche or Greek Yogurt
- Spray Oil
- 10–12 capers with a lemon juice squeeze
- 4 rolls of bread or 8 thin slices of bread

Directions:

1. Warm up the air-fryer to 200°C (390°F).

2. Combine the oil, vinegar, salt, and pepper in a bowl. Add some sliced zucchini to the sauce. Fry for an hour in the air at 200 degrees. needs to be shaken periodically. Serve.

46. Cornbread with Pulled Pork

Prep & Cook: 50mins

Servings: 6

Ingredients:

- 2 ½ Mugs shredded pork (leftover works well too)
- small amount of dried rosemary
- A half-teaspoon of chili powder
- (3) cloves peeled and pressed garlic
- a half recipe Pancake Mix (from a box)
- 0.5 tablespoons of brown sugar
- Scallions, thinly sliced; 1/3 mug.
- sea salt.

Directions:

3. Heat a large nonstick skillet on medium. Sauté sliced scallions and pressed garlic until fragrant.
4. Add dried rosemary, chili powder, brown sugar, and salt to pulled pork. Boil while stirring occasionally.
5. Preheat the air fryer to 335°F (168 degrees Celsius). Spray two small loaf pans with oil.
6. The loaf pans should evenly distribute pulled pork mixture.

7. Cornbread batter should be made as directed on the box and dropped over seasoned pulled pork.
8. Cornbread should be cooked in a preheated air fryer for 18 minutes, or until a toothpick inserted in the center comes out clean.
9. Enjoy your flavorful cornbread with pulled pork!

47. Fish Finger Sandwich

Prep & Cook: 36 mins

Servings: 4

Ingredients:

- 4 Tiny Cod Fillets (Skin Take off)
- Salt and Pepper, to Taste
- Two tablespoons flour
- 40g Dried Breadcrumbs
- In a 250g spray oil, add frozen peas and a tablespoon of crème fraiche or Greek yogurt.
- 10–12 Capers Lemon Juice
- 8 Small Bread Slices or 4 Bread Rolls

Directions:

1. Pre-heat your air fryer.
2. Each cod fillet should be lightly seasoned with salt and pepper, then dusted with flour before being rolled in breadcrumbs.
3. Use a spray can to coat the bottom of the air fryer's basket. The coated cod fillets should be baked for 15 minutes at 200 degrees Celsius (or 390 degrees Fahrenheit).

4. Prepare the frozen peas by boiling them in water while the fish is in the oven. The peas should be drained before being blended with crème fraiche, capers, and lemon juice.

5. Assemble your fish sandwich on bread pieces or rolls after the fish is done cooking. Add toppings like lettuce and tartar sauce, then top with a layer of fish fingers and pea puree.

6. Enjoy your delicious fish finger sandwich!

48. Zucchini Chips

Prep & Cook: 75 mins

Servings: 6

Ingredients:

- 4 Zucchinis, thinly sliced
- Seasoning of your choice
- 2 tablespoonful Salad-oil
- 2 tablespoonful Balsamic Vinegar.

Directions:

1. Whisk the balsamic vinegar, salad oil, salt, and pepper together in a bowl until a smooth consistency is achieved.

2. After adding the zucchini slices to the mixture, toss them to ensure that they are evenly coated.

3. While the zucchini slices are cooking in the air fryer at a temperature of 200 degrees Fahrenheit, shake the basket once (93 degrees Celsius). One hour is spent cooking.

4. Once the zucchini slices are crisp and golden, take off them from the air-fryer and serve. Enjoy your zucchini chips!

49. Apple Chips

Prep & Cook: 25 mins

Servings: 1

Ingredients:

- 1 Apple, cored and cut into half-moon slices
- 1/4 teaspoonful Cinnamon
- Pinch of Salt and Sweetener

Directions:

1. Sprinkle the apple slices with cinnamon, salt, and sweetener.
2. Apple slices should be seasoned before being placed in the basket of an air fryer that has multiple levels.
3. After attaching the lid, select the "air fry" setting on the air fryer's control panel. Cooking apple slices requires 390 degrees Fahrenheit (199 degrees Celsius) for a total of 12 minutes, including one flip halfway through the process.
4. Serve your crispy and flavorful apple chips.

Prep & Cook: 50 mins

Servings: 4

Ingredients:

- 3 Chicken Breasts
- 1 medium bag Frozen Vegetables of Choice
- 1 Mug Cooked Rigatoni or Pasta of Choice
- Paprika
- Garlic and Herb Seasoning
- Italian Dressing
- Black Pepper
- Ground Parsley
- Oil Spray

Directions:

1. Season chicken breasts with paprika, garlic, herb, and a tablespoon of Italian dressing. Add ground parsley and black pepper. Spray oil on seasoned chicken breasts in the air-fryer. Cook 15 minutes at 360°F (182°C).
2. Turn the chicken over and season the other side with pepper and parsley after half the cooking time. Respray the food with oil spray and cook until done.
3. While the chicken is cooking, season a bag of frozen vegetables with garlic and herb dressing and Italian dressing in a vessel. Mix well.
4. Cook the seasoned vegetables in the air-fryer at 380°F (193°C) for 12 mins.
5. Dice the cooked chicken and season it with garlic and herb seasoning, parsley, and Italian dressing.

6. Mix the diced chicken with the cooked pasta and vegetables, adjusting seasoning to taste.
7. Serve your chicken pasta salad and enjoy!

51. Black Bean and Tater Tots

Prep & Cook: 35 mins

Servings: 3

Ingredients:

- 1 1/4 mugs Tater Tots
- 1 mug Black Beans
- Salsa
- Dairy-Free/Vegan Sour Cream
- Garlic Lemon Sauce (see recipe below)

Directions:

1. Prepare the air fryer at 400°F (200 degrees Celsius). Shake the air fryer basket after 7 minutes and add black beans and tater tots. Cook for 5 more minutes to tenderize the tator tots and heat the beans.
2. Preheat the oven to 425♦♦F. (220 degrees Celsius). Put potato tots on a parchment-lined baking sheet. After 15 minutes, lower the oven to 375°F (190 degrees Celsius). Turn infants to keep them in one layer.
3. While the tator tots fry, slice the green onions and make the garlic lemon sauce.
4. To assemble, pile cooked tater tots on plates, top with black beans, salsa, dairy-free sour cream, and garlic lemon sauce. Garnish with green onions and serve immediately.

Garlic Lemon Sauce:

5. Combine a sprinkle of salt, chopped garlic, and the juice and zest of one lemon. Quantities may be adjusted to suit individual preferences.

52. Bourbon Peach Wings

Prep & Cook: 50 mins

Servings: 6

Ingredients:

- ½ mug Peach Preserves
- 1 tablespoon Brown Sweetener
- 1 Garlic Clove, minced
- 1/4 teaspoonful Salt
- 2 tablespoonful White Vinegar
- 2 tablespoonful Bourbon
- 1 teaspoonful Cornstarch
- 1-1/2 teaspoonful Fuls Water
- 2 pounds Chicken Wings

Directions:

1. Preheat the air fryer to 400°F (200°C).
2. In a food processor, combine salt, brown sugar, garlic powder, and peach preserves. Transfer to a pot and heat while adding white vinegar. Simmer the sauce for 4-6 minutes, or until it slightly thickens.
3. Stir cornstarch and water into a smooth paste in a different bowl before adding it to the preserves. In order to thicken, lower the heat to a low simmer and whisk for one to two minutes. Set aside one-fourth of the sauce.

4. Discard the wing tips after cutting the chicken wings through the joints. The wing pieces should be arranged in a single layer in the cooking spray-coated air fryer basket. Turn the food over and baste the other side with the sauce you saved after 6 minutes. To ensure browning and doneness, cook for an additional 6 to 8 minutes.
5. Serve the wings with the reserved sauce.

53. Coconut Chicken Tenders

Prep & Cook: 50 mins

Servings: 3

Ingredients:

- 2 Huge Eggs
- 2 teaspoonfuls Garlic Powder
- teaspoonful Salt
- 1/2 teaspoonful Black Pepper
- 3/4 mug Panko Breadcrumbs
- 3/4 mug Grated Sweet Coconut
- 1 pound Chicken Tenders
- Cooking Spray

Directions:

1. the air fryer to 400 degrees Fahrenheit before using it (200 degrees Celsius). A large baking sheet should be covered with oil spray.
2. In a wide, shallow dish, beat the eggs with the garlic powder, along with the salt and pepper.

3. Panko breadcrumbs and shredded coconut should be mixed together in a separate, shallow dish.

4. Chicken tenders are dipped in egg, then coated with the breadcrumb-coconut mixture and pressed to provide a good coating.

5. Spread chicken tenders with their coating on the baking sheet. Cooking spray should be used on the tops.

6. Air frying the tenders for 12 to 14 minutes will produce chicken that is cooked through and a coating that is crisp and golden in color.

7. Serve your coconut chicken tenders with your favorite dipping sauce.

54. Cottage Cheese -Stuffed Chicken Breast

Prep & Cook: 65 mins

Servings: 2

Ingredients:

- a half of a cup of cottage cheese
- 2 eggs, beaten 2 chicken breasts of medium size, cut in half.
- tablespoons of fresh coriander, chopped.
- teaspoon of fine sea salt seasoned breadcrumbs
- Black pepper, freshly ground, one-third teaspoonful three cloves, garlic, minced very finely.

Directions:

1. Use a meat tenderizer to press the chicken breasts flat.

2. Combine the cottage cheese, garlic, coriander, salt, and pepper in a mixing bowl.

3. One chicken breast should be topped with one-third of the mixture, and you should repeat with the remaining ingredients.
4. Use toothpicks to hold the filling inside the chicken roll.
5. Eggs are beaten in a sizable mixing bowl. Combine the seasoned breadcrumbs, salt, and black pepper in a different shallow dish.
6. After dipping the chicken breasts in the beaten egg, coat them in breadcrumbs.
7. At 365°F (185°C), cook the stuffed chicken breasts in the air fryer for 22 minutes.
8. Serve the cottage cheese-stuffed chicken breasts immediately.

55. Honey Glazed Chicken

Prep & Cook: 40 mins

Servings: 3

Ingredients:

- 7 Skinless, Boneless Chicken Thighs
- 1/2 Mug Runny Honey
- 1/2 Mug Worcestershire Sauce
- 1/2 Mug Tomato Sauce
- 1 1/2 teaspoonful Fuls Fresh Crushed Garlic
- 1/2 teaspoonful Ground Ginger
- 4 portions of Steamed Wild Rice
- 1 Small Onion, finely chopped
- Seasoning of your choice

Directions:

1. Warm up the air-fryer to 390°F (200°C).

2. Place the chicken thighs in the air-fryer and cook for 25 mins until fully cooked and crispy.
3. Meanwhile, prepare the honey glaze by mixing honey, Worcestershire sauce, tomato sauce, crushed garlic, and ground ginger in a saucepan. To make a little thicker sauce, bring to a boil, then decrease heat to a simmer and cook for 4-6 minutes.
4. Season the honey glaze with salt and black pepper to taste.
5. Once the chicken is cooked, brush the honey glaze over the crispy chicken thighs.
6. Serve the honey glazed chicken over steamed wild rice and garnish with finely chopped onion.

56. Thai Mango Chicken

Prep & Cook: 35 mins

Servings: 2

Ingredients:

- Mixed herbs chicken seasoning
- ½ mango peeled and diced
- Seasoning of your choice
- Spicy chicken seasoning
- tsp red Thai curry paste
- tbsp salad-oil
- 1 lime rind and juice
- 2 chicken breasts

Directions:

1. Ensure that your Air-fryer is Warm uped to 355 F.
2. Make a mixture of your mixed herbs sea-soning, mango, salt, pepper, spicy chicken seasoning, Red Thai Curry Paste, salad-oil, and lime into a clean mixing vessel. En-sure that you mix thoroughly so that the seasoning is evenly distributed in the mix-ture.
3. With the aid of your vegetable knife, cut slightly into your chicken without the cut reaching the bottom of the breasts.
4. Sprinkle the seasoning mixture in the mixing vessel and ensured that sufficient seasoning gets into the cuts.
5. Transfer the sprinkled chicken into your air-fryer, on the baking mat. Set the timer for 15 mins and allow to cook. Always check well to ensure that the chicken is well-cooked in the center.
6. Garnish some fresh tomatoes and extra lime, and serve with the cooked chicken.

57. Shrimp Stroganoff

Prep & Cook: 25mins

Servings: 4

Ingredients:

- 1 tbsp butter
- medium onion, grated
- lb. of medium clean shrimp
- Salt and pepper
- 4 tbsp of brandy
- 3 ½ oz. minced pickled mushrooms
- 3 tbsp of tomato sauce
- tbsp of mustard
- 1 can of cream

Directions:

1. The shrimp should be cleaned. Remove the peels and thoroughly wash them with water and lemon, then drain and set aside.
2. Brown the onion in the butter. Remove from the heat and stir in the shrimp, seasoning with salt and pepper.
3. Put in air-fryer at 3200F for 5 mins.
4. Heat the cognac in a shell until it catches fire. And transfer it over the shrimp, flaming them.
5. Add the mushroom, tomato sauce, mustard, and put back in the air-fryer for about 5 mins.
6. When serving, add the cream, stir well and heat without boiling.
7. Serve the stroganoff with white rice and straw potatoes.

Chapter 8:

Dessert Recipes

58. Cocoa Banana Brownies

Prep & Cook: 45 mins

Servings: 12

Ingredients:

- Two Mugs almond flour
- teaspoonful Fuls baking powder
- teaspoonful baking powder
- ½ teaspoonful baking soda
- ½ teaspoonful salt
- 1 over-ripe banana

- Three huge eggs
- ½ teaspoonful stevia powder
- ¼ Mug coconut oil
- tablespoon vinegar
- Mug almond flour.
- One third Mug cocoa powder

Directions:

1. Turning on the air fryer and letting it run for five minutes will get it ready to use.
2. Blend or process everything in a food processor until it is completely smooth.
3. Place in an air fryer-compatible baking dish.
4. Cook for thirty minutes at 350 degrees Fahrenheit in the air fryer basket, or until a toothpick inserted in the center comes out clean.

59. Coffee Cake

Prep & Cook: 25 mins

Servings: 2

Ingredients:

- egg
- tsp cocoa powder
- 1/4 Mug flour
- 1/4 Mug sweetener
- 1 tbsp black coffee
- 1/2 tsp instant coffee
- 1/4 Mug butter

Directions:

1. Spray some cooking spray into a miniature baking dish, then set it aside.
2. Egg, butter, and sweetener are beaten together in a separate container. After adding the black coffee, instant coffee, and cocoa powder, give the mixture a good beating.
3. After adding the flour, mix thoroughly to combine.
4. Place the batter in the baking dish that you will be using.
5. Arrange a baking dish on top of the steam rack and slide it into the air fryer.
6. Place air-fryer cover on pot, choose bake mode, and program oven to 330 degrees Fahrenheit and 15 minutes.
7. Enjoy your meal.

60. Toffee Cookies

Prep & Cook: 22 mins

Servings: 8

Ingredients:

- 1 egg
- 1/3 Mug toffee chips
- 1/2 cooking powder
- Mug all-purpose flour.
- tsp vanilla
- 1/2 Mug brown sweetener
- 4 tbsp butter, softened.
- salt

Directions:

1. In a mixing bowl, combine the butter and sweetener and beat until smooth.
2. Add the vanilla extract and egg to the mixture.
3. Combine the baking soda, flour, and salt in a mixing bowl.
4. Toss in some toffee chips and mix well. Refrigerate cookie dough for at least an hour.
5. Insert the dehydrating tray into the air fryer's multi-tiered basket.
6. Prepare a parchment paper-lined dehydrating tray.
7. Bake some cookies using the dough and set them on the dehydrator rack.
8. Set the air fryer's cover on and the timer for 9 minutes with the temperature at 350 degrees Fahrenheit.
9. Put the remaining cookies through the same baking process.

61. Quick Oatmeal Cake

Prep & Cook: 50 mins

Servings: 8

Ingredients:

- 2 huge eggs
- 1 Mug powdered sweetener
- 1 Mug brown sweetener
- 1/2 Mug margarine
- 1 1/2 Mugs flour
- 1 tsp vanilla extract
- tsp baking soda
- ground cinnamon
- ½ Mugs warm water.

- 1 Mug quick oats
- salt

Directions:

1. Prepare the baking dish by greasing it with butter and setting it aside.
2. The sixth open spot on the rack should be filled with a wire rack. Decide whether to bake, then set the oven to 350 degrees, and set the timer for 40 minutes. Press the start button to start the oven heating up.
3. Combine the steaming water and the instant oats. From the possible options, eliminate.
4. Sweetener, brown sugar, and margarine should be mixed thoroughly in a sizable mixing bowl.
5. In a sizable mixing bowl, combine the flour, salt, cinnamon, baking soda, vanilla, and eggs.
6. Mixing the oats with the water before adding them to the batter is recommended.
7. Bake the dish for forty minutes after transferring the batter into the prepared baking dish.
8. Slice and serve.

62. Spiced Walnut Mugcakes

Prep & Cook: 25 mins

Servings: 2

Ingredients:

- Egg yolk
- tablespoonsful chopped Walnuts.

- 1/8 teaspoonful Vanilla
- 1 tablespoon Sour cream
- 2 tablespoonsful melted Butter.
- 3 tablespoonful Maple syrup
- 3 tablespoonful Milk
- 1/8 teaspoonful Ground cinnamon
- 1/2 teaspoonful baking powder
- 2 tablespoonful Brown sweetener
- ½ Mug All-purpose flour.
- teaspoonful Salt

Directions:

1. Cooking spray two ramekins, then set them aside. In a medium bowl, combine the flour, cinnamon, baking powder, brown sugar, and salt.
2. Combine the egg yolk, vanilla, sour cream, butter, maple syrup, and milk in a separate bowl. The flour and egg mixture should be thoroughly combined.
3. Mix in chopped walnuts. Fill ramekins with batter.
4. The air fryer's multi-tiered basket should hold the dehydrating tray. Place ramekins in a dehydrator. Cover the pot with air fryer cover.
5. Bake at 380 F for 15 minutes in bake mode. Serve.

63. Vegan Chocolate Vanilla Bars

Prep & Cook: 17 mins

Servings: 12

Ingredients:

- 1 Mug sweetener free and vegan chocolate chips

- 2 tablespoonful coconut butter
- 2/3 Mug coconut cream
- 2 tablespoonful stevia
- ¼ teaspoonful vanilla extract

Directions:

1. Put the cream in a vessel, add stevia, butter and chocolate chips and stir
2. Leave aside for 5 mins, stir well and mix the vanilla.
3. Turn on your air fryer, spread the mixture out on a baking sheet lined with parchment paper, and cook for 7 minutes at 356 degrees F.
4. Slice and serve the mixture after it has had time to cool.
5. Enjoy!

64. Banana Foster

Prep & Cook: 20 mins

Servings: 1

Ingredients:

- tablespoon unsalted butter
- 2 teaspoonfuls dark brown sweetener
- banana, peeled and halved lengthwise and then crosswise.
- 2 tablespoonful chopped pecans.
- ⅛ teaspoonful ground cinnamon
- 2 tablespoonful light rum
- Vanilla ice-cream, for serving.

Directions:

1. Combine the brown sweetener and butter in a round heat-proof pan that measures 6 inches in diameter and 3 inches in height. Place the pan inside the basket of the air fryer.
2. In an air fryer preheated to 350 degrees Fahrenheit, melt the butter along with the sweetener for two minutes. To combine the ingredients, stir them together.
3. After adding the pecans and banana pieces, turn the mixture to coat everything.
4. Banana chunks are ready after five minutes in an air fryer set to 350 degrees Fahrenheit and one flip.
5. Cinnamon should be sprinkled on top. Take the pan out of the air fryer and put it somewhere safe, like the back of the stove where it will be dark.
6. In a saucepan, combine the rum, butter, and sugar.
7. Light the sauce carefully with a long-reach lighter. While bananas are burning, pour sauce over them. Put it on ice cream.

65. Dark Rum Cake

Prep & Cook: 40 mins

Servings: 6

Ingredients:

- ½ package yellow cake mix
- 3.4-ounce package Jell-O instant pudding
- Two eggs
- ¼ Mug of vegetable oil
- ¼ Mug of water
- ¼ Mug dark rum

Directions:

1. Put all of the ingredients into the vessel and use an electric mixer to mix them together until they are completely incorporated.
2. After greasing a square baking dish measuring 8 inches on all sides, line the bottom with a piece of parchment paper.
3. At this point, you should wrap the cake pan in aluminum foil.
4. Spread the mixture into the pan that has been prepared, and then use the back of the spoon to even it out.
5. Prepare the cooking chamber of the Air-fryer Plus Air-fryer Oven by placing the drip pan in its lowest position.
6. Turn the thermostat to 325 degrees Fahrenheit and choose the "Air Dry" option.
7. Put 25 minutes on the timer and hit "Start."
8. When it says "Add Food" on the screen, swap the baking pan and drip pan positions.
9. Do nothing when the screen reads "Turn Food."
10. Remove the pan from the Air-fryer and let it cool on a wire rack for 10 minutes.
11. For best results, wait until the cake has cooled completely before slicing it.
12. Cut into desired-sized slices and serve.

66. Marshmallow Turnovers

Prep & Cook: 20 mins

Servings: 4

Ingredients:

- Four sheets of defrosted filo pastry
- Four tablespoonsful of chunky peanut butter
- Four teaspoonfuls of marshmallow fluff

- 2 ounces of melted butter
- Seasoning of your choice

Directions:

1. Warm up your Air-fryer to a temperature of 360 degrees Fahrenheit (182 °C)
2. Take one of your filo sheets and brush it up with butter.
3. On top of your filo sheet, place another sheet and butter it up as well.
4. Keep repeating until all leaves are used up.
5. Mug the stalks into three pieces of 3x12 inch strips.
6. Take about one tablespoon of peanut butter and marshmallow fluff and add them under your filo strips.
7. Hold the sheet and fold it over your mixture, forming a triangle, and then keep folding it in a zigzag manner until all of the fillings has been wrapped up.
8. Take some butter and tighten.
9. Add the sheets to your cooking basket and cook for about 3-5 mins.
10. Serve with a sprinkle of salt.

67. Lemon Blueberry Cake

Prep & Cook: 55 mins

Servings: 6-8

Ingredients:

- 2 Mugs unbleached all-purpose flour
- 2 tsp. baking powder
- egg room temp
- tsp. vanilla extract
- ½ Mug buttermilk

- 2 Mugs blueberries
- 1/2 lemon juice
- 1/2 Mug powdered sweetener
- Seasoning of your choice
- 1 lemon zest
- 1/2 Mug unsalted butter room temp
- 3/4 Mug sweetener

Directions:

1. Grease and flour a dish for Air-fryer.
2. Mix the flour, baking powder, and saltin a vessel.
3. Reserve 2 tablespoonful of mixture.
4. Blend zest, sweetener, egg, vanilla, and room temperature butter.
5. Add flour mixture and buttermilk to the sweetenered butter in the stand mixer.
6. Mix blueberries with reserved flour and add to batter.
7. Transfer water in Air-fryer with rack.
8. Spoon half of the batter into the greased dish in the Pot.
9. Set Air-fryer to high pressure for 30 mins.
10. Mix the half lemon juice with half Mug powdered sweetener and transfer over cake.
11. Repeat with the second cake and serve.

Prep & Cook: 45 mins

Servings: 6

Ingredients:

- Doughnuts:
- 1 1/4 mug all-purpose flour
- 1/3 cup sweetener
- teaspoon baking powder
- teaspoon baking soda
- ¾ teaspoon salt
- Egg
- mug buttermilk
- 1/2 teaspoon vanilla
- 2 tablespoons melted, cooled unsalted butter
- tablespoon melted butter for toppings
- Filling:
- 1/2 cup blueberry or strawberry jelly (not preserves)
- Glaze: 1/2 mug powdered sweetener
- Tbsp milk
- Two tablespoons peanut butter
- A pinch of sea salt

Directions:

1. Donuts with a peanut butter glaze that are air fried. In a large bowl, combine the ingredients for the cake: flour, sweetener, baking powder, baking soda, and salt.

2. In four separate bowls, whisk together egg, melted butter, buttermilk, and vanilla.

3. Create a well in the middle of the dry ingredients, then pour in the water. First combine the ingredients using a fork, then switch to a large spoon and continue stirring as you add the flour.

4. Place the dough in a work area that has been dusted with flour. Keep in mind that it will be sticky in the beginning. After carefully combining the ingredients, the dough should be pressed to a thickness of about three quarters of an inch. Use a cutter with a diameter of 3 1/2 inches to cut circles out of the dough, and then brush them with melted butter. After placing each ball of dough on a piece of baking paper, they should be placed in the air fryer. If your fryer is on the smaller side, you will need to work in batches.

5. Fry at a temperature of 350 degrees for 11 minutes. To fill each doughnut with jelly, you can either use a squeeze bottle or a pastry sac.

6. Mix the ingredients for the glaze in a bowl using a whisk, then spread it on top of each doughnut.

69. Ham and Tomatoes Mix Appetizer

Prep & Cook :14mins

Servings: 3

Ingredients:

- Ham (chopped) – 2 tbsp.
- Grated cheese – 2 mugs
- Flour – 2 mugs
- Tomatoes (chopped) – 2
- Parsley (chopped) – 1 mug
- Milk – 1 mug

- Oil – 1 tbsp.
- Egg – 1

Directions:

1. Put some oil into the air fryer's pan.
2. Collect together the ham, flour, tomatoes, milk, egg, salt, and parsley.
3. Hold at 300 degrees for 10 minutes.
4. Add cheese as a finishing touch when serving.

70. Chocolate Cake In An Air Fryer

Prep & Cook: 25mins

Servings: 5

Ingredients:

- spray for cooking
- ¼ cup of regular sugar
- 3 and a half tablespoons of butter, one egg that has been whisked.
- one tablespoon of apricot jam.
- a tablespoon of unsweetened cocoa powder and six tablespoons of all-purpose flour

Directions:

1. Prepare an air fryer by heating it to 320 degrees Fahrenheit (160 degrees C). Spray some cooking spray into a miniature tube pan with flutes.
2. A bowl of sugar and butter should be mixed with an electric mixer until fluffy and light. Mix the egg and jam well. Sift the flour, cocoa powder, and salt and

mix well. Pour the batter into the prepared pan. Smooth the batter with the back of a spoon.

3. Put the pan in the air fryer basket. A cake is done when a toothpick inserted into the middle comes out clean after 15 minutes.

Conclusion

Congratulations! Congratulations, you've reached the final page of our cookbook! And if you already have some tried-and-true recipes for the Air Fryer, jot them down, fire up the appliance, and get ready to do some frying in the Air Fryer!

The ever-increasing number of people who are having issues with their health has led to the necessity of the air fryer. The use of excessive oil in food is contributing to a number of health problems that are becoming increasingly life-threatening, including high cholesterol levels, cardiac disorders, and obesity. Because of this, traditional frying has been condemned by the society of health experts, and they all recommend eating food that has a lower percentage of oil and fat content. The invention of the air fryer was a boon for people who were having trouble cutting down on the amount of fat they consumed on a daily basis. A kitchen miracle, an Air Fryer is capable of frying food to a super-crispy texture while requiring very little oil to do so.

This compact cooking vessel is available in a wide range of sizing and design options. In addition, every model has a unique assortment of cooking options and a control panel. Air fryers are electric appliances that are considered to be energy efficient due to the technology that enables them to cook food in a short amount of time while achieving excellent results.

In addition to that, it is an excellent appliance for producing healthy food that is crisp without the use of oil. They reduce the amount of effort you need to put into frying because the appliances come equipped with temperature sensors, a cooking timer, and a heating element that controls the temperature. When using an Air Fryer to prepare food, there is a significantly decreased risk of the food catching fire or being cooked unevenly. Additionally, a smaller number of cooking utensils are needed to prepare a variety of foods when using an air fryer. You are able to prepare a full meal using this appliance, including vegan recipes, steaks, crusted chicken and seafood, breakfast, and even desserts. This is in addition to the fact that you are able to make crispy fries and snacks using this appliance. Because of the Air Fryer's adaptability, it's a handy appliance to have around the house when you're cooking. Whether you are a novice in the kitchen or a seasoned professional, the appliance will assist you in preparing a wide range of mouthwatering treats for the table. If you use an air fryer, you will also be able to perform other types of cooking, such as baking, roasting, broiling, and poaching, amongst a great many others. This is made possible by its 10 in 1 technology, which operates in a manner analogous to that of an oven and a fryer.

The recipes that are provided in each chapter are designed to be followed by any level of cook, from someone who has never cooked before to an experienced chef.

You can finally give the trend of air frying a shot and see for yourself whether or not you were convinced that it was too good to be true when it first became popular. Your food will have the crispiness of deep-fried food with only a tablespoon or two of oil when you use this miraculous appliance. If you have this appliance in your kitchen, you won't need to go to county fairs or seek out fast food restaurants to indulge in fried delicacies; this is because frying food at home results in a healthier meal.

If you own an air fryer but were unsure of what to make in it before, you won't have that problem anymore thanks to this collection of recipes that covers all meals of the day, from breakfast to dessert.

What exactly are you holding out for at this point? You can start enjoying all the foods you thought were unhealthy once you start cooking with your air fryer.

Printed in Great Britain
by Amazon

36856178R00059